$12.00

591.594 McDonnell, Janet
MCD   Animal builders

ANIMAL BUILDERS

by Janet McDonnell

Created by

THE CHILD'S WORLD

Distributed by CHILDRENS PRESS®
Chicago, Illinois

The publisher wishes to thank the following for the use of their drawings and photographs: Erwin & Pegg Bauer/BRUCE COLEMAN INC., cover; Mike Blair, 31 (bottom); Patrice Ceisel/John G. Shedd Aquarium, 39; David H. Funk, 41; (C.H. Greenewalt)/VIREO, 43; Jerry Hennen, 9 (bottom); Steven Holt, 7; Karen Jacobsen, 11 (top), 31 (top); (M.P. Kahl)/VIREO, 23; Thomas D. Mangelsen/Images of Nature, 5 (right); Murphy/Jahn, Architects, 5 (left); Dieter & Mary Plage/BRUCE COLEMAN INC., 15; Mike Price/BRUCE COLEMAN INC., 21; James P. Rowan, 11 (bottom); Leonard Lee Rue III, 35; Alan Singer, 19, 25, 29, 33; Lynn M. Stone, 9 (top), 17, 27, 47; Tom J. Ulrich, 37; Jan L. Wassink, 45; J.A.L. Watson, 13. cover design by Kathryn Schoenick

Library of Congress Cataloging-in-Publication Data

McDonnell, Janet, 1962-
  Animal builders / by Janet McDonnell.
    p. cm. — (Amazing animal facts)
  Includes index.
  Summary: Discusses the habitations built by such animals as the paper wasp, trap-door spider, weaverbird and beaver.
  ISBN 0-89565-511-X
  1. Animals—Habitations—Juvenile literature.
[1. Animals—Habitations.] I. Title. II. Series.
QL756.M36   1989
591.59'4—dc19   88-36641 CIP AC

CHILDRENS PRESS HARDCOVER
EDITION   ISBN 0-516-06386-3

CHILDRENS PRESS PAPERBACK
EDITION   ISBN 0-516-46386-1

1 2 3 4 5 6 7 8 9 10 11 12 R 97 96 95 94 93 92 91 90 89

ANIMAL
BUILDERS

Grateful appreciation is expressed to Mark Rosenthal, curator for the Lincoln Park Zoo, Chicago, for his assistance in insuring the accuracy of this book.

Human beings have built some wonderful things. Skyscrapers, subways, and bridges are just a few. But we aren't the only expert builders on the planet. Many animals have also shown amazing talent as builders.

Animals build for many reasons, just as humans do. They build homes to protect themselves and their young from bad weather and enemies. They build traps to catch food and build places to store food. Animals build things to help them survive.

Left: Northwestern Atrium Center, Chicago
Right: Masked weaverbird weaving nest

Tiny Builders: Insects & Spiders

Some of the most amazing animal builders are also the tiniest: insects and spiders. The most famous insect builders are probably the honeybees. They are well known for their carefully built wax homes, called honeycombs. Honeycombs are made out of beeswax, which the bees make in their bodies. It takes a lot of food and energy for the bees to make wax. So they use as little wax as possible in building a honeycomb. The bees build hexagonal (six-sided) cells that all fit perfectly together. Every wall of wax is used by two cells.

To make the honeycomb, the bees chew the wax to soften it. Then they mold it into shape. Hundreds of bees work together to make the honeycomb. Then they use the cells for storing their honey and raising their young. Bees build their honeycombs in hollow trees or in wooden boxes provided by beekeepers.

Hornets also build nests with hexagonal cells. But hornets cannot make wax in their bodies. Instead, they use wood to make paper for building.

In the spring, the queen hornet builds a few cells to lay her eggs in. Using her strong jaws, she scrapes bits of wood from fence posts, old boards, or dead trees. She chews the wood into a pulp by adding her saliva. Then she spreads out the pulp in thin layers and shapes it into cells with her mouth and legs. The pulp dries into a paper so strong that you could even write or type on it!

The queen lays one egg in each cell. The eggs hatch and the hornets grow. When the hornets are old enough, they help to add to the nest. The queen keeps laying eggs in the new cells.

The hornets enclose the nest in layers of paper. You might not think much of a paper roof. But it protects the hornets' nest from rain and changing temperatures.

The award for the largest insect nest would surely go to the termites. These tiny insects can build nests that are twenty feet tall! A nest that big takes many years to build. It is home for several million termites.

Most termites mix soil and saliva to build their nests. The mixture dries as hard as brick. The walls of these nests, called *termitaries*, can be two feet thick!

Termites build their nests to protect themselves. Most kinds of termites do not like light. They have soft, pale bodies. If they stay out in the sun too long, they will die. Termites need to live in a dark, warm, and humid place, so they build one!

They also need, like all animals, to breathe fresh air. Inside the thick walls of the nest, the termites build an "air-conditioning" system. Ducts and tunnels run along areas in the walls that have many small holes. Fresh air comes in through the holes and stale air goes out.

Arrows show air flow inside termitary.

Termitaries come in many shapes, depending upon where they are built. In tropical rain forests, termites build umbrella-like roofs on top of their nests. The roofs protect the nests from heavy rains.

But in the treeless lands of Australia, the nests look completely different. They look like tombstones. Why? The sun is so hot there, it could bake the termites inside their nests. To avoid that disaster, the termites always build their nests so the flat, wide sides face the east and west. Therefore, only the narrow sides of the nests catch the intense rays of the midday sun. That is why the nests don't overheat.

These termites are called compass termites, and you can guess why. But scientists are still confused by how the termites know east and west. Compass termites are blind!

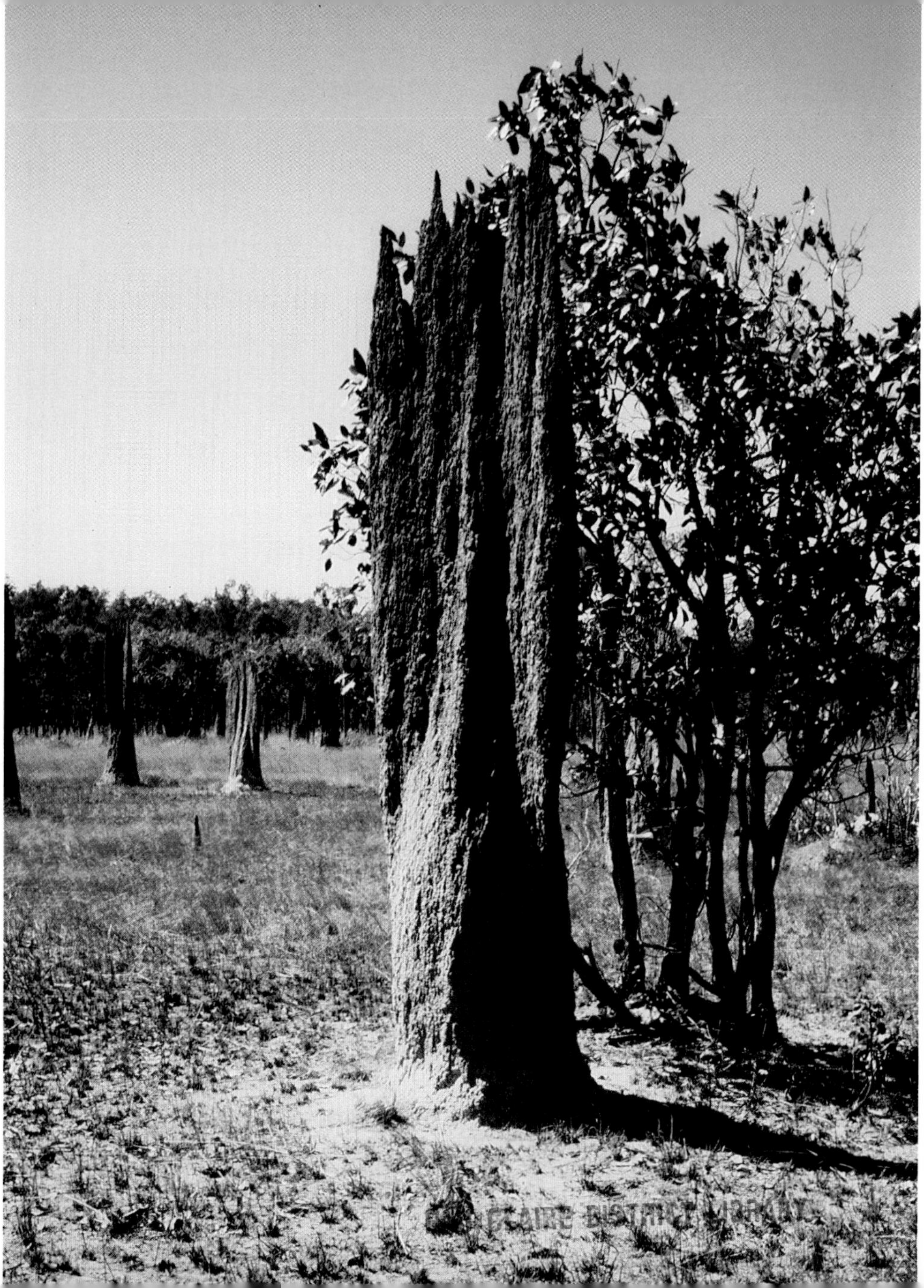

Weaver ants build nests much smaller than those of the compass termites. But they are just as amazing. You may think that all ants live in the ground. Not so. Weaver ants live high in the trees of tropical forests. And they "sew" leaves together for their nests.

The ants search for two or more leaves growing close to each other or for one large leaf. A group of ants pulls two leaf edges together. Then another team of ants joins in. In this team, each adult ant holds a larva in its jaws. Larvae are the helpless, just-hatched ants. They cannot see or crawl yet. But they can often make silk.

The adult ant strokes and squeezes the larva to make it produce silk. Holding the larva, the ant zigzags between the two leaf edges. The adult ant and the larva "sew" the leaves together with silk!

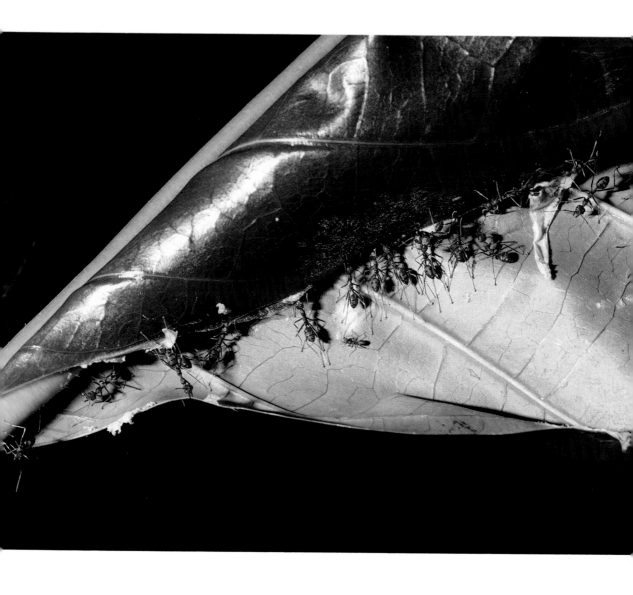

The trap-door spider builds a very different kind of trap. This spider uses its jaws to dig a tube in the soil. It then lines the walls of the tube with silk to make them stronger. Next, the spider makes a lid for the tube.

There are two kinds of lids. One is made by spinning a thin layer of silk over the entrance. Then the spider piles dirt and moss over the door to hide it. The spider bites around the edges of the door, leaving a hinge. The other type of door is more like a cork. It is also made with silk and soil. But it is thick and fits snugly over the entrance.

The trap-door spider uses its tube as a nest, a hiding place, and a trap. The spider either waits in the tube until it feels the vibrations of a passing insect, or it lifts the door just a bit and waits there for a victim. The trap-door spider attacks with lightning speed. It quickly poisons the victim. Then the spider drags it into the tube and eats in privacy.

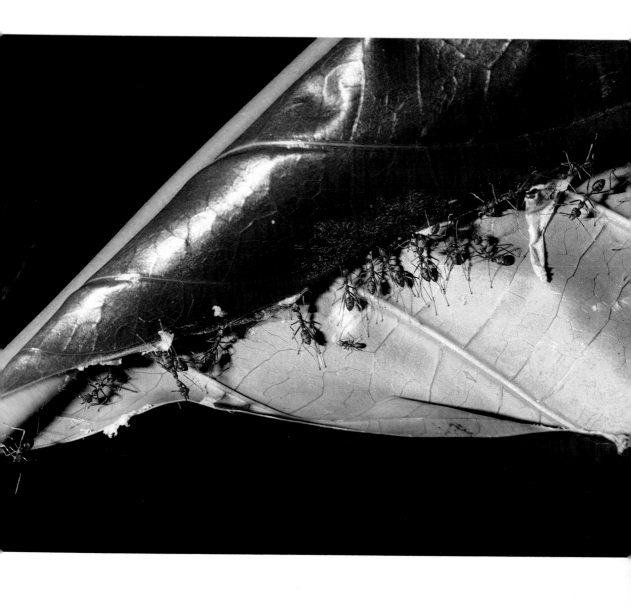

Spiders also use silk to build. Most spiders can make several different kinds of silk. They can make silk that is thick or thin. They can also make it sticky or dry. The silk comes out of tiny tubes, called *spinnerets*, in the spider's abdomen.

Different kinds of spiders build different kinds of webs. The kind that you have probably seen most often is called an orb web. The spokes of the orb web are made with dry silk. The spiral part is made with sticky silk to trap insects. But before the spider lays out the sticky silk, it lays out a path in dry silk. The dry silk acts as a guide. The spider goes back over the same spiral path, eating the dry silk and spinning sticky silk behind it.

Then the spider sits in the center of the web and waits for dinner to arrive. When an insect is trapped on the sticky threads, it sends vibrations to the center of the web. Then the spider knows it's suppertime!

The trap-door spider builds a very different kind of trap. This spider uses its jaws to dig a tube in the soil. It then lines the walls of the tube with silk to make them stronger. Next, the spider makes a lid for the tube.

There are two kinds of lids. One is made by spinning a thin layer of silk over the entrance. Then the spider piles dirt and moss over the door to hide it. The spider bites around the edges of the door, leaving a hinge. The other type of door is more like a cork. It is also made with silk and soil. But it is thick and fits snugly over the entrance.

The trap-door spider uses its tube as a nest, a hiding place, and a trap. The spider either waits in the tube until it feels the vibrations of a passing insect, or it lifts the door just a bit and waits there for a victim. The trap-door spider attacks with lightning speed. It quickly poisons the victim. Then the spider drags it into the tube and eats in privacy.

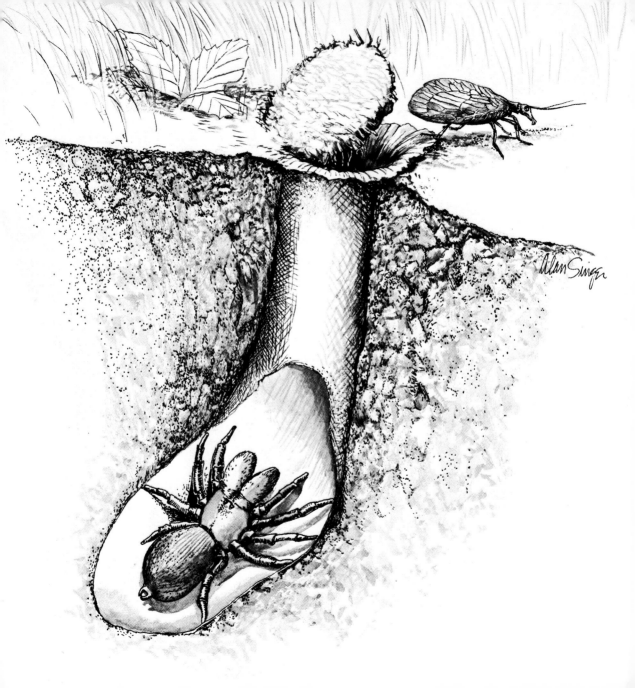

Bird Builders

Birds' nests are very important to them. They must be strong, warm, and safe to protect the eggs and, later, the baby birds. But some birds build nests that are more than just useful. They are amazing.

One of these birds is the weaverbird. The male weaverbird uses his beak to weave strips of grass into a basket-like nest. He can even tie knots! Some nests have an entrance tube at the bottom. It protects the eggs from hungry tree snakes because the snakes cannot crawl up the tubes.

The male weaverbird has to do a good job on his nest, because his nest is what attracts a female. If a female likes the nest, she will line the inside with soft materials. Then the two will mate. But if the male cannot attract a female, he destroys his nest and starts all over again.

In places where there are few trees, weaverbirds may live together in a sort of "bird apartment"! These birds are called sociable weavers. One tree may be home for over one hundred birds.

The roof of the giant nest acts as an umbrella to keep out the rain. Underneath the roof, each pair of birds has its own nest. Sometimes the nest is so huge, the tree branches break under its weight and the nest crashes to the ground!

Unlike the weaverbird that weaves its nest, the tailorbird sews its nest. The tailorbird sews together leaves to make a cup. Using its long, pointed beak for a needle, the tailorbird pokes holes in the edges of the leaves. For thread, the tailorbird uses stolen spiderwebs, pieces of bark, or other handy materials.

Once the leaves are sewn together, the inside is stuffed with soft, warm materials such as animal hair and thistledown. The finished nest is safe and cozy for baby birds.

Alan Singer

The cactus wren's nest is very safe too, but it sure doesn't look cozy! This bird usually builds its nest in the arms of a deadly cactus. The sharp cactus needles act as a sort of barbed-wire fence against enemies. But the cactus wren somehow manages to hop around on the cactus without being hurt.

The wren's nest is domed and has a tunnel entrance. It acts as a year-round shelter for the whole family. When the baby birds grow older, they build their own nests.

Birds' nests can be made of many things, such as grass, leaves, and mud. But one type of bird, the cave swiftlet, uses a very strange material—its own saliva. These little birds live mainly in the caves of Asia. They build their nests high up against the cave walls, using their sticky saliva, which hardens in the air. It takes five to six weeks to finish a nest.

But after all the birds' hard work, men with long poles often knock the nests down. Why? Believe it or not, the swiftlets' nests are the main ingredient in something called bird's nest soup! The nests often sell for a lot of money. But no one pays the birds!

Alan Singer

Though harvest mice do not build whole towns, they are still considered expert builders. In fact, they may be the best of the mammal builders.

Like the weaverbirds, harvest mice use long strips of grass to tightly weave small, ball-shaped nests. The mice usually build their nests in fields. The nests often hang between tall grass stems which are woven into the nests. The quick-climbing mice use the stems as ladders, too.

The inside of each nest is lined with soft things like pieces of fur. The nest is a safe, warm place for the mice to have their babies. But as time goes on, the grass used to weave the nest dries out. The nest becomes loose. When the baby mice are about two weeks old, they begin to tear the nest apart. Then it's back to work for the parents. They must build a new nest before they have another litter.

Alan Singer

Mammal Builders

Although most birds build nests, not many mammals are builders. Of the mammals that do build, most make their homes underground. Prairie dogs go a step further. They build whole "towns."

Prairie dogs live in large groups in places called prairie dog towns. They build the towns by digging underground tunnels and rooms. The rooms each have a purpose. A few feet under the entrance hole is the listening post. When the prairie dogs see danger, they jump into their holes. Then they go to the listening post. There they listen to find out if the danger is gone. Farther down the hole, prairie dogs build a nesting room for new litters.

The prairie dogs pile the dirt they dig out of the tunnels into mounds around the entrance holes. The mounds are very important. Prairie dogs stand on top of them to watch for enemies. The mounds also keep flood waters out of the tunnels.

*Prairie dog town
underground*

Though harvest mice do not build whole towns, they are still considered expert builders. In fact, they may be the best of the mammal builders.

Like the weaverbirds, harvest mice use long strips of grass to tightly weave small, ball-shaped nests. The mice usually build their nests in fields. The nests often hang between tall grass stems which are woven into the nests. The quick-climbing mice use the stems as ladders, too.

The inside of each nest is lined with soft things like pieces of fur. The nest is a safe, warm place for the mice to have their babies. But as time goes on, the grass used to weave the nest dries out. The nest becomes loose. When the baby mice are about two weeks old, they begin to tear the nest apart. Then it's back to work for the parents. They must build a new nest before they have another litter.

Alan Singer

Perhaps the most famous mammal builders are the beavers. Beavers are known for the dams and lodges they build. They build them to protect themselves. Beavers are clumsy and slow on land, but they can swim very fast. That's why they like to stay near water, where they can make a quick escape if they need to.

The beavers build dams in streams to back up water and make deep ponds. To make a dam, they push large branches into the mud on the bottom of the stream. They weigh the branches down with rocks. Then they pile on more layers of sticks and stones and leaves. The beavers then plug up any holes with mud.

Most dams are about three feet high and a few hundred feet long. Some of them are strong enough for a horse to cross!

Once a dam is finished, a lodge is built. First the beavers pile up mud from the bottom of the stream to make an island. Then they pile on branches and twigs. Next, the beavers pack mud all over the pile, except at the very top. They leave a small hole at the top so they will be able to breathe. Finally, the beavers go underwater and chew two or more tunnels into the middle of the pile. Then they clear out a small room in the middle. The room is just above water level.

The lodge keeps the beavers safe throughout winter. No enemies can get inside. The mud freezes solid. But the beavers can get out. The dam makes a pond so deep, it never freezes all the way to the bottom. So the beavers can swim through the tunnels to get to the food they have stored on the bottom of the pond.

Underwater Builders

As you might imagine, it is very difficult to build things underwater. Of all the many underwater animals, only a few build nests. One of the best-known examples is the stickleback fish. The male stickleback builds a nest to attract females.

There are several kinds of stickleback nests. The one shown on page 39 is made by the male wrapping pieces of weeds around two stems. Next the fish sprays a sticky substance that he makes in his kidneys over the nest to hold it together. Then he tunnels through the nest with his body.

When a female comes to the male, he coaxes her into the tunnel with his head. She enters the nest, and the male nudges her tail to get her to lay eggs. After she is done, the male slips into the nest and fertilizes the eggs. Many females may lay their eggs in the same male's nest. The stickleback nest is a busy place!

Another underwater builder is the caddisworm. When it is fully grown, it becomes a caddis fly. But until it becomes a fly, the caddisworm lives in the water.

The caddisworm is in trouble right from the start of its life. It has a very soft and, to most fish, delicious lower body. So, as soon as the worm hatches, it begins to build a protective covering for itself. Just like the weaver ant larva, the caddisworm can make silk in its body. The silk acts as a glue to hold together things like sand and pieces of shells to make a case.

Some caddisworms that live in fast-flowing streams use heavy stones in their cases. The stones act as anchors. One kind of caddisworm makes its case with twigs sticking out in all directions. That makes it hard for a fish to swallow the worm. There are many kinds of caddisworm cases. Some people even collect them!

Interior Decorators

Some animals are not happy just to build things. They decorate too! The best-known animal decorators are the bowerbirds of Australia and New Guinea. The male bowerbird builds a walkway, or bower, of twigs and grass on the forest floor. Then he decorates it to attract a female.

There are several kinds of bowerbirds. Each kind decorates differently. Spotted bowerbirds collect bones of small animals to decorate the ground in front of their bowers. Satin bowerbirds usually like blue objects. Some even "paint" the walls of their bowers. They crush berries and rub the bluish juice on the walls.

When a female bowerbird is near, the male dances in front of the bower to attract her. He picks up objects in his beak to show her. If she likes his decorating job, they will mate.

Pack rats (or bushy-tailed woodrats) are also animal decorators. They build loose nests of sticks and grass in the mountains and deserts.

For some reason, pack rats like to collect glittery objects. They pick up broken glass, coins, spoons, mirrors — anything that glitters. Sometimes they steal shiny things from nearby farmhouses or campers and leave sticks or stones in their place! It may seem like the pack rat has made a trade. But the truth is that pack rats often drop what they're carrying when they find something better. The pack rats usually litter the shiny objects around the front of their nests.

Now you have seen how talented animals can be. You have seen animal decorators, weavers, tailors, and sculptors. They use skills that many believe only humans have. But that's not so. From twenty-foot termitaries to tiny, delicate spiderwebs, animals build some amazing things. And if you keep your eyes wide open, you may see some of these expert builders at work.

Red-headed woodpecker making a home

INDEX